First Facts™

Water All Around

Sources of Water

by Rebecca Olien

Consultant:
Peter R. Jaffé, Professor
Department of Civil and Environmental Engineering
Princeton University
Princeton, New Jersey

Capstone press

Mankato, Minnesota

First Facts is published by Capstone Press,
151 Good Counsel Drive, P.O. Box 669, Mankato, Minnesota 56002.
www.capstonepress.com

Library of Congress Cataloging-in-Publication Data
Olien, Rebecca.
    Sources of water / by Rebecca Olien.
    p. cm.—(First facts. Water all around)
    Includes bibliographical references and index.
    ISBN 0-7368-3700-0 (hardcover)
    ISBN 0-7368-5180-1 (paperback)
    1. Water—Juvenile literature. I. Title. II. Series.
GB662.3.O575 2005
551.46—dc22   2004011459

Summary: A description of the earth's water sources, salt water, and freshwater.

Editorial Credits
Christine Peterson, editor; Linda Clavel, designer; Ted Williams, illustrator; Kelly Garvin,
    photo researcher; Scott Thoms, photo editor

Photo Credits
Bruce Coleman Inc./Mark Newman, cover
Cindy Ruggieri, 14
Corbis/Ariel Skelley, 19; M.ou Me. Desjeux, Bernard, 20
Gilbert S. Grant, 4–5, 7, 8–9, 10
Image Ideas, 13
Photodisc Royalty Free, 15
Tom Stack & Associates Inc./Thomas Kitchin, 11

1 2 3 4 5 6 10 09 08 07 06 05

Table of Contents

Water Covers
the Earth

Earth is called the "water planet." Water covers about 70 percent of the planet. It fills oceans, lakes, and rivers. Water soaks into the ground. It collects under the ground in **aquifers**. It is frozen in **glaciers**. Life on the earth depends on many sources of water.

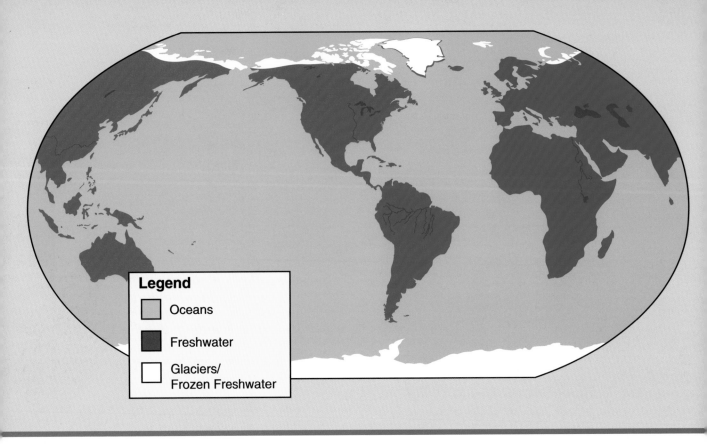

Legend
- ☐ Oceans
- ■ Freshwater
- ☐ Glaciers/ Frozen Freshwater

Where Is Water Found?

Most of the earth's water is salt water found in oceans. **Salt water** makes up 97 percent of all water. Only 3 percent is **freshwater**.

Most freshwater is frozen in glaciers.
Rivers and lakes hold a small amount
of freshwater. The ground also stores
some freshwater.

Oceans and Seas

Water found in oceans and seas is salty. It contains salt and minerals. People can't drink salt water.

In some areas, people have little freshwater to drink. They get drinking water from the ocean. They take out the salt so ocean water is safe to drink.

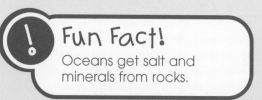

Fun Fact!
Oceans get salt and minerals from rocks.

Water as Ice

Mountains and polar areas hold a small amount of the planet's water. Snow that falls in these areas does not melt. It packs together and turns into ice.

Packed ice and snow become glaciers.
Glaciers cover large areas of land.
Chunks of glacier ice break off into the
ocean. They form icebergs.

Lakes and Ponds

Freshwater collects in lakes and ponds. Lakes and ponds are sources of water for many animals. Rain and snow add water to lakes. Rivers often flow into and out of lakes.

! Fun Fact!
Lake Vostok lies under a thick sheet of ice in Antarctica.

Rivers and Streams

Rivers and streams carry water. Rain and melted snow flow into rivers as **runoff**. Water seeps into rivers and streams from the ground.

Rivers are important water sources.
Animals drink freshwater from rivers.
Most people in cities get drinking water
from rivers.

Precipitation

Dirt and rock

Groundwater aquifer

Surface water

Groundwater

Groundwater flows under the ground. **Precipitation** seeps into the ground. Water trickles down inside cracks and spaces in rock. Water then collects in underground aquifers. People drill wells to reach groundwater.

Fact!
The ground holds more freshwater than all the world's lakes and rivers.

Water Sources Cover Earth

Sources of water are everywhere. Water falls as rain. It fills lakes and rivers. Frozen glaciers hold freshwater as ice. Oceans are filled with salt water. People, plants, and animals use water from all of these sources.

Lake Baikal in Russia holds at least 20 percent of all the fresh surface water in the world. It holds as much freshwater as all of the U.S. Great Lakes combined. Lake Baikal is the world's deepest lake. The lake is 5,315 feet (1,620 meters) deep.

Hands On: Groundwater

The ground holds more freshwater than all the lakes and rivers on the earth. Have an adult help you try this activity to see how water collects under the ground.

What You Need

scissors
clear plastic 2 quart (2 liter) bottle
modeling clay
1 cup (240 mL) small rocks
1 cup (240 mL) gravel

1 cup (240 mL) sand
1 cup (240 mL) soil
pin
paper cup
1 cup (240 mL) water

What You Do

1. Cut the top off of the plastic bottle.
2. Flatten the clay on the bottom of the bottle.
3. Layer the following items in the bottle, starting at the bottom: rocks, gravel, sand, and soil. These layers represent the earth's layers.
4. Use a pin to poke holes in the bottom of the paper cup.
5. Hold the cup over the plastic bottle.
6. Pour water in the cup. Let the drops "rain" on the layers in the bottle.
7. Watch how the water flows through each layer and collects in the bottom of the bottle. Groundwater flows through the earth's layers in the same way.

Glossary

aquifer (AK-wuh-fuhr)—an underground lake

freshwater (FRESH-wah-tur)—water that has little or no salt; most ponds, rivers, lakes, and streams have freshwater.

glacier (GLAY-shur)—a large sheet of frozen freshwater; glaciers are found in mountains and polar areas.

groundwater (GROUND-wah-tur)—water that is found underground

precipitation (pri-sip-i-TAY-shuhn)—water that falls from clouds to the earth's surface in the form of rain, snow, sleet, or hail

runoff (ruhn-AWF)—water that flows over land instead of soaking into the ground

salt water (SAWLT WAH-tur)—water that is salty; salt water is found in oceans.

Read More

Nadeau, Isaac. *Water in Glaciers.* The Water Cycle. New York: PowerKids Press, 2003.

Royston, Angela. *Oceans.* My World of Geography. Chicago: Heinemann, 2005.

Ryan, William T. *World of Water.* Science Links. Philadelphia: Chelsea Clubhouse, 2003.

Internet Sites

FactHound offers a safe, fun way to find Internet sites related to this book. All of the sites on FactHound have been researched by our staff.

Here's how:
1. Visit *www.facthound.com*
2. Type in this special code **0736837000** for age-appropriate sites. Or enter a search word related to this book for a more general search.
3. Click on the **Fetch It** button.

FactHound will fetch the best sites for you!

Index